JUN 0 8

Forbidden City

CASTLES, Palaces & TOMBS

China's Imperial Palace

By Barbara Knox

Consultant: Stephen F. Brown, Director
Institute of Medieval Philosophy and Theology, Boston College

BEARPORT
PUBLISHING COMPANY, INC.

New York, New York

Credits

Cover, Panorama Stock Photos Co Ltd / Alamy; title page, Panorama Stock Photos Co Ltd / Alamy. Background image (throughout), ChinaStock; pages 4–5, SCPhotos / Alamy; 6, National Palace Museum, Taiwan, Republic of China; 7, 8, ChinaStock; 9, British Library Images Online; 11, 12, 13, ChinaStock; 14, ChinaStock; 15, Hu Weibiao / www.agefotostock.com; 16, Steve Skjold / Alamy; 17, Liu Liqun / ChinaStock; 18, ChinaStock; 19, The Art Archive / British Museum; 20, Hu Weibiao / www.agefotostock.com; 21, Dean Conger/CORBIS; 22, Wood / Hulton Archive / Getty Images; 23, Hulton Archive / Getty Images; 24–25, AP / Wide World Photos; 25, Time Life Pictures / Pix Inc. / Time Life Pictures / Getty Images; 26–27, Rodica Prato; 28, Pixtal / www.agefotostock.com; 29, Panorama Stock Photos Co Ltd / Alamy.

Original design and production by Dawn Beard Creative, Triesta Hall of Blu-Design, and Octavo Design and Production, Inc.

Library of Congress Cataloging-in-Publication Data

Knox, Barbara.
  Forbidden City : China's imperial palace / by Barbara Knox.
    p. cm. — (Castles, palaces & tombs)
  Includes bibliographical references and index.
  ISBN 1-59716-070-9 (library binding)—ISBN 1-59716-107-1 (pbk.)
 1. Forbidden City (Beijing, China)—Juvenile literature. 2. China—Kings and rulers—Biography—Juvenile literature. I. Title: China's imperial palace. II. Title. III. Series.

DS795.8.F67K66 2006
951'.156—dc22

2005029608

For more information, write to Bearport Publishing Company, Inc., 101 Fifth Avenue, Suite 6R, New York, New York 10003. Printed in the United States of America.

1 2 3 4 5 6 7 8 9 10

Table of Contents

A Wonderful Dream

The **monk** lay quietly sleeping. Suddenly, he jumped up out of bed. He walked quickly back and forth in his small room. He'd just had a strange yet wonderful dream.

In his dream, he saw a shining city glowing with light. Buildings trimmed in gold rose up behind a great red wall. The **emperor** sat on a magnificent throne.

The monk hurried from his room. He ran to tell his **pupil**, Yung Lo, about his dream. He knew the dream meant Yung Lo would one day become emperor of China. He would build a great palace city.

In ancient times, the Chinese believed that dreams could tell the future.

Tiananmen Gate is the main gate to the Forbidden City.

A Fierce Father

Yung Lo's father, Hung Wu, ruled over China. He was very cruel. Hung Wu beat palace servants with big sticks. He chopped off the heads of people who brought him bad news. In 1380, he killed more than 30,000 people who had plotted to steal his throne.

Emperor Hung Wu

Hung Wu taught his 24 sons to be fierce fighters. He wanted Yung Lo and his brothers to help him protect China. When Yung Lo was just ten years old, he was crowned Prince of Yen. His father gave him the city of **Beijing** to rule.

Today, Beijing is a busy city with a population of over 14 million people.

Hung Wu ruled China from 1368 to 1398. He was the first ruler of the Ming **dynasty**.

The Black Dragon

By the time Yung Lo was 20 years old, he led a great **army**. His soldiers fought the **Mongols** who lived north of China. Yung Lo soon became as cruel as his father. He was also hungry for power.

When Yung Lo's **nephew** was named emperor, Yung Lo gathered his army. He rode to **Nanking** and burned down his nephew's palace. Yung Lo announced that he was the new emperor of China.

A sculpture of the Chinese army during the Ming dynasty

Yung Lo became known as the "Black Dragon." He killed the people who worked for his nephew. Then he killed their families. Yung Lo was hated and feared by the Chinese people.

Yung Lo

In 1402, Yung Lo became the third emperor of the Ming dynasty.

Building the Dream

Yung Lo never forgot the monk's dream. When he finally became emperor, he decided to build a great palace in Beijing. Surrounding this palace would be a big city. It would be the largest palace city in the world. He would call it the Forbidden City.

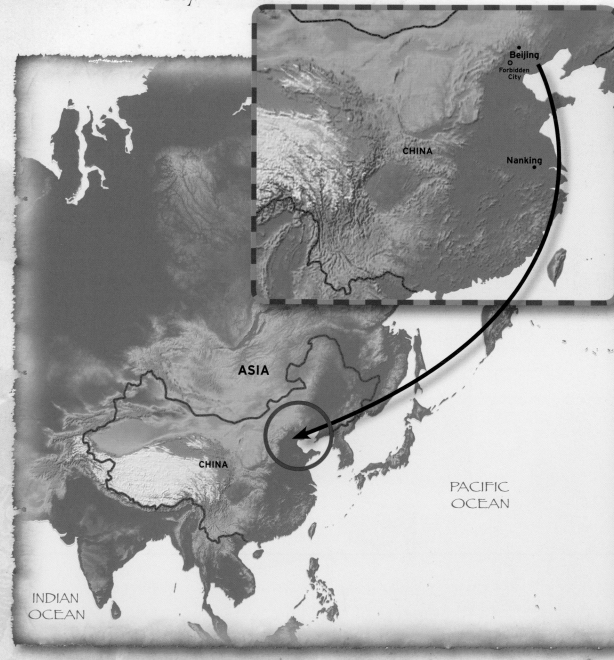

More than one million **slaves** and prisoners were needed to build the city. Yung Lo's soldiers rode into China's villages and **kidnapped** the townspeople. Then they forced them to work on the palace.

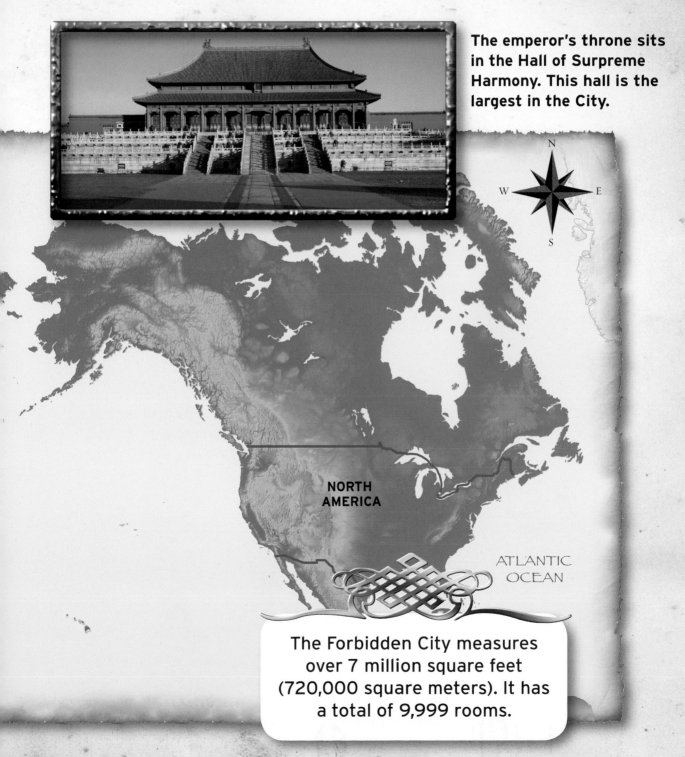

The emperor's throne sits in the Hall of Surpreme Harmony. This hall is the largest in the City.

NORTH AMERICA

ATLANTIC OCEAN

The Forbidden City measures over 7 million square feet (720,000 square meters). It has a total of 9,999 rooms.

Made of Rice and Eggs

Building the palace city was difficult. The slaves had to think of clever ways to make their work easier. To move huge pieces of stone to the building site, they dug **wells** along the road. In the winter, they took water from the wells and poured it onto the road. Soon the road was covered with ice. Workers then slid the stones along the ice and into the Forbidden City.

Slaves also built most of the Great Wall of China during the Ming dynasty.

Workers also made millions of bricks for the walls. They mixed sticky rice and **lime** to form the bricks. Then they mixed egg whites and rice to make cement. The rice-and-egg walls were as hard as rock when they dried.

The Hall of Medium Harmony (building on the left) is where emperors rested before major ceremonies.

Workers started building the Forbidden City in 1406. Yung Lo moved into the City in 1421.

Looking South

The Forbidden City sits inside a great wall 33 feet (10 m) high. Beautiful towers rise from each of the four corners. A **moat** surrounds the wall. The wall and moat kept enemy soldiers out.

All the main buildings face south. In the 1400s, the Chinese considered this direction good luck. They believed money, health, and happiness came from the south.

One of the towers surrounded by the moat

At the same time, the Chinese people feared that the north was a place where evil came from. Only one building in the palace faced north. When one of the women made the emperor mad, he punished her by sending her to stay in that building.

An aerial view of the Forbidden City

The Forbidden City is filled with many good-luck symbols such as deer, flowers, fruit, butterflies, and birds.

Danger in the Shadows

More than 10,000 people lived in the Forbidden City. The emperor had a grand palace all his own. His many wives lived nearby, in separate buildings. Even his children had their own palaces. The Forbidden City also had schoolrooms, two theaters, and hundreds of gardens.

One of the many gardens

Danger often lurked in the City's shadows. The emperor's wives fought with one another. The servants stole treasures. Guards chopped off the heads of anyone caught breaking the rules. One time, one of the emperor's wives was thrown down a well for making him mad.

A theater in the Forbidden City

In 1425, the Forbidden City had 6,300 cooks. They made more than 30,000 meals a day.

Fire!

Over the years, the emperors prayed to the fire gods to protect the Forbidden City. Fire, however, often swept through the wooden buildings.

In the 1500s, the emperor's palace burned to the ground. His family was inside celebrating the **harvest**. Thousands of candles hung from the walls. Ladies wearing silk dresses carried lanterns strung on poles. Suddenly, a gust of wind blew through the hall. Sparks flew everywhere. Soon a roaring fire filled the palace. The emperor ran for his life.

In the 1500s, the Palace of Heavenly Purity burned down.

The next day, the emperor ordered that the palace be rebuilt. He wanted it to be even more beautiful than before.

A silk painting of the Forbidden City in the 1500s

In 1653, the emperor's palace burned again. It was rebuilt within three years.

Filled with Treasures

Twenty-four emperors lived in the Forbidden City between 1421 and 1911. Each emperor added more treasures to the city.

Emperor Wan Li, who ruled in the 1600s, loved beautiful things. He ordered workers to create gold plates, jeweled vases, and silver lanterns. He filled his palaces with silk pillows, fur blankets, and **jade** statues. He was more interested in his treasures than in taking care of his people.

The golden throne in the Hall of Supreme Harmony

When the emperors ran out of money, they made the poor villagers pay more **taxes**. Then they spent the money buying more treasures for the Forbidden City.

Some treasures found in the Palace of Heavenly Purity

The emperor and his wives ate from solid gold plates and bowls.

The End of Emperors

In 1911, the Chinese Revolution swept the country. People did not want to be ruled by emperors anymore. The gates of the Forbidden City were thrown open. People streamed in to see the wonders of the city for the first time.

**The entrance to the Forbidden City in 1908,
a few years before the Chinese Revolution**

In 1937, war with Japan broke out. Officials quickly packed up the treasures of the Forbidden City. They moved almost 3,000 crates to safety in Taipei, Taiwan. Many of those pieces were never returned. Today, a museum in Taipei displays many of the City's finest treasures.

People leaving Shanghai, China, during the war with Japan.

The Hall of Preserving Harmony includes a collection of some of the oldest pieces of artwork in the Forbidden City.

Change for China

In 1949, life changed again for the Chinese people. The 1949 revolution, led by Mao Tse-tung, brought **communist** rule to the country. China became known as the People's Republic of China.

People gather in Tiananmen Square on October 1, 2005.

Today, the Chinese celebrate important events in front of the Forbidden City. Thousands of people gather in Tiananmen Square, which is the largest open area in Beijing. There, on October 1, a celebration is held to honor Mao Tse-tung and the beginning of the People's Republic of China. The days of the Forbidden City's **imperial** rulers are long past.

Mao Tse-tung in 1940

Until he died in 1976, Mao Tse-tung lived near the Forbidden City, in a small house with a yellow roof. In Yung Lo's time, only the emperor's palaces had yellow roofs.

Visiting the Forbidden City

Almost eight million people visit the Forbidden City in Beijing every year. Today it is called the Palace Museum. Visitors enter through the Meridian Gate. In Yung Lo's time, only the emperor could walk through this gate.

When the emperor sat on the throne, everyone else in the palace had to lie facedown on the floor. Then they would shout, "Long live your majesty!"

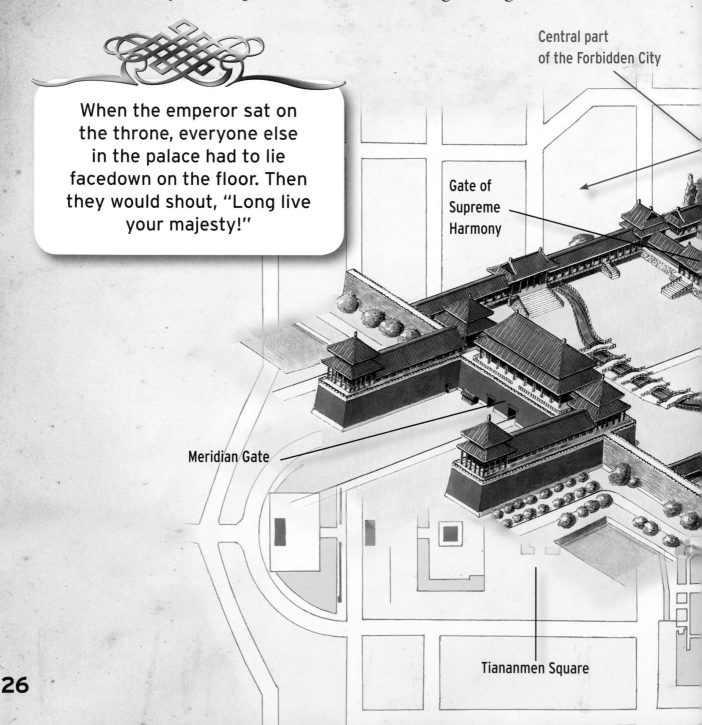

Central part of the Forbidden City

Gate of Supreme Harmony

Meridian Gate

Tiananmen Square

Many tourists go straight to the Hall of Supreme Harmony. There, a golden throne sits between tall golden **pillars**. Dragons decorate the pillars and the ceiling. The doors have dragon handles. Six hundred years ago, the Black Dragon himself sat upon the throne. The monk, who once dreamed such a beautiful dream, stood nearby.

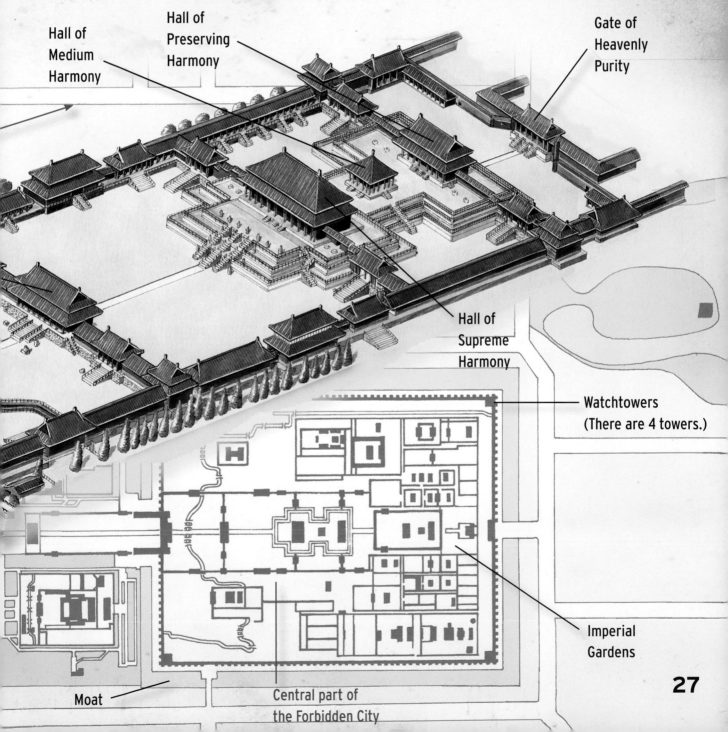

Hall of Medium Harmony

Hall of Preserving Harmony

Gate of Heavenly Purity

Hall of Supreme Harmony

Watchtowers (There are 4 towers.)

Imperial Gardens

Moat

Central part of the Forbidden City

Just the Facts

❧ Nine is considered a lucky number by the Chinese. This is the reason there are 9,999 rooms in the Forbidden City.

❧ All the buildings in the City are made of painted wood. At one time, to help put out fires, large metal pots filled with water were placed throughout the buildings.

❧ The Forbidden City was also called the Purple Forbidden City, or the Great Within.

❧ Only the emperor and his wives were allowed to wear yellow.

Inside the Palace of Heavenly Purity

Timeline

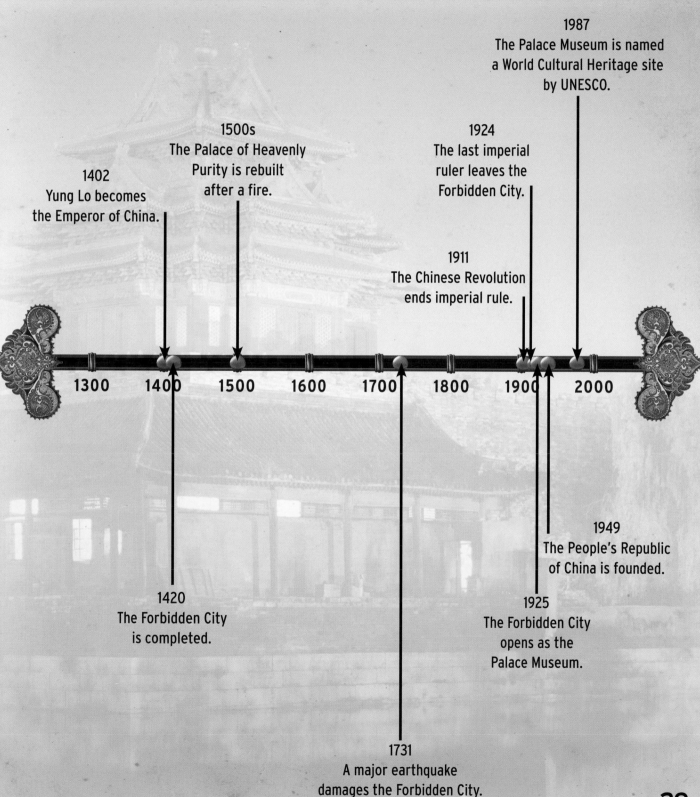

1402
Yung Lo becomes
the Emperor of China.

1500s
The Palace of Heavenly
Purity is rebuilt
after a fire.

1987
The Palace Museum is named
a World Cultural Heritage site
by UNESCO.

1924
The last imperial
ruler leaves the
Forbidden City.

1911
The Chinese Revolution
ends imperial rule.

1300 1400 1500 1600 1700 1800 1900 2000

1420
The Forbidden City
is completed.

1949
The People's Republic
of China is founded.

1925
The Forbidden City
opens as the
Palace Museum.

1731
A major earthquake
damages the Forbidden City.

Glossary

army (AR-mee) a group of people who have been trained to fight

Beijing (bay-JING) the capital of China, also known as Peking

communist (COM-yuh-nist) a person who supports a type of government where the government owns all goods and property

dynasty (DYE-nuh-stee) a group of rulers from the same family

emperor (EM-pur-ur) a man who rules a country

harvest (HAR-vist) the season when crops are gathered

imperial (im-PIHR-ee-uhl) having to do with an empire or its ruler

jade (JAYD) a green mineral used for making jewelry and ornaments

kidnapped (KID-*napped*) captured someone and kept the person as a prisoner

lime (LIME) a white powder made from limestone that's used to make plaster and cement

moat (MOHT) a deep, wide ditch dug around a castle and filled with water to prevent attacks

Mongols (MOHN-guhlz) people who were part of the Muslim empire that ruled India from 1526–1857

monk (MUHNGK) a religious man who has devoted his life to prayer and teaching

Nanking (NAN-king) the old capital of China

nephew (NEF-yoo) the son of someone's brother or sister

pillars (PIL-urz) tall posts that are part of a building

pupil (PYOO-puhl) a young student

slaves (SLAYVZ) people who are forced to work for another person for no pay

taxes (TAKS-es) money paid by people to the ruler of a country

wells (WELS) deep holes dug in the ground to get water

Bibliography

Chan, Charis. *Imperial China.* London, England: Penguin Books (1991).

Dorn, Frank. *The Forbidden City: The Biography of a Palace.* New York: Charles Scribner's Sons (1970).

MacFarquhar, Roderick. *The Forbidden City.* New York: Newsweek Book Division (1972).

Read More

Czernecki, Stefan. *The Cricket's Cage.* Winnipeg: Hyperion Press (1997).

Harvey, Miles. *Look What Came from China.* London, England: Franklin Watts (1999).

Nash, Deborah. *Made in China.* London, England: Frances Lincoln (2004).

Schroeder, Holly. *China ABCs: A Book About the People and Places of China (Country ABCs).* Mankato, MN: Picture Window Books (2004).

So, Sungwan. *C Is for China.* London, England: Frances Lincoln (2004).

Zemlicka, Shannon. *Colors of China.* Minneapolis, MN: Carolrhoda Books (2001).

Learn More Online

Visit these Web sites to learn more about the Forbidden City:

www.beijingtrip.com/attractions/forbidden/

www.ebeijing.gov.cn/Tour/ScenicSpots/t20040812_156829.htm

www.encyclopedia.com/html/Y/Yunglo.asp

Index

About the Author

Barbara Knox has written about Dracula's castle in Romania
and the great American palace, Hearst Castle.
She lives in Minneapolis, Minnesota, with her daughter, Annie.